ALL GOD'S CHILDREN

ALL GOD'S CHILDREN

Photographs by Shelley Langston / Text by Hubert I. Bermont

STEIN AND DAY / *Publishers* / New York

Consider this proposition.

We adults muck things up.

Adolescence is a halfway house.

But as children our responses to the world . . .

. . . are direct.

Children make friends easily

even if cautiously.

They can be with themselves without feeling lonely.

*Even when they go their
separate ways together.*

They don't count calories

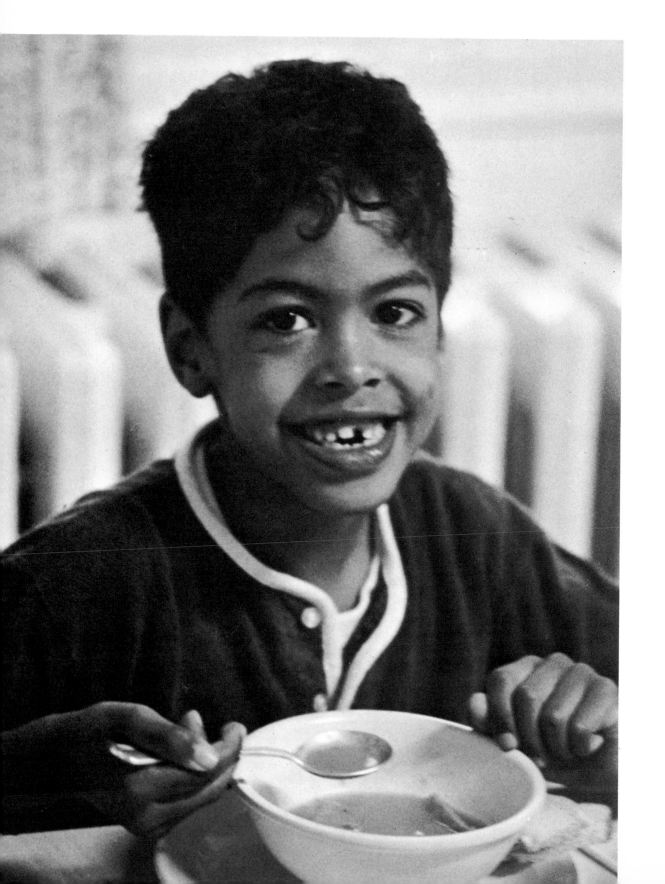

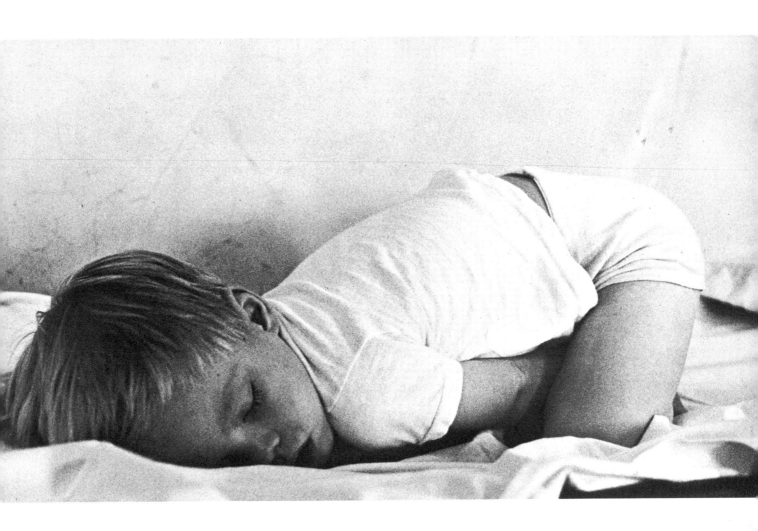

They sleep without pills

They are reasonably well-balanced.

They try harder.

*They even stop to thin[k]
once in a whi[le]*

They shouldn't envy us.

We should envy them.

*They don't need
many possessions.*

They fall in love with simple things.

Their curiosity . . .

. . . is endless.

*Their quarrels with their environment
can sometimes be remedied in ten seconds,*

or five.

They can establish a community

They can construct something terribly important.

*They can create something
that didn't exist before.*

The world is full of wonders.

Like spacemen,
they can look over
the edge of the world

and be astonished by the size of it all

While not neglecting the elements . . .   *air . . .*

Fire . . .

Earth . . .

Water.

True, children have problems also.

They sometimes look down when they should be looking up

They can be difficult . . .

*They spend time
keeping up with the Joneses.*

nd they have to figure out
hat to do with what they've got.

But there are so many
distracting pleasures around,

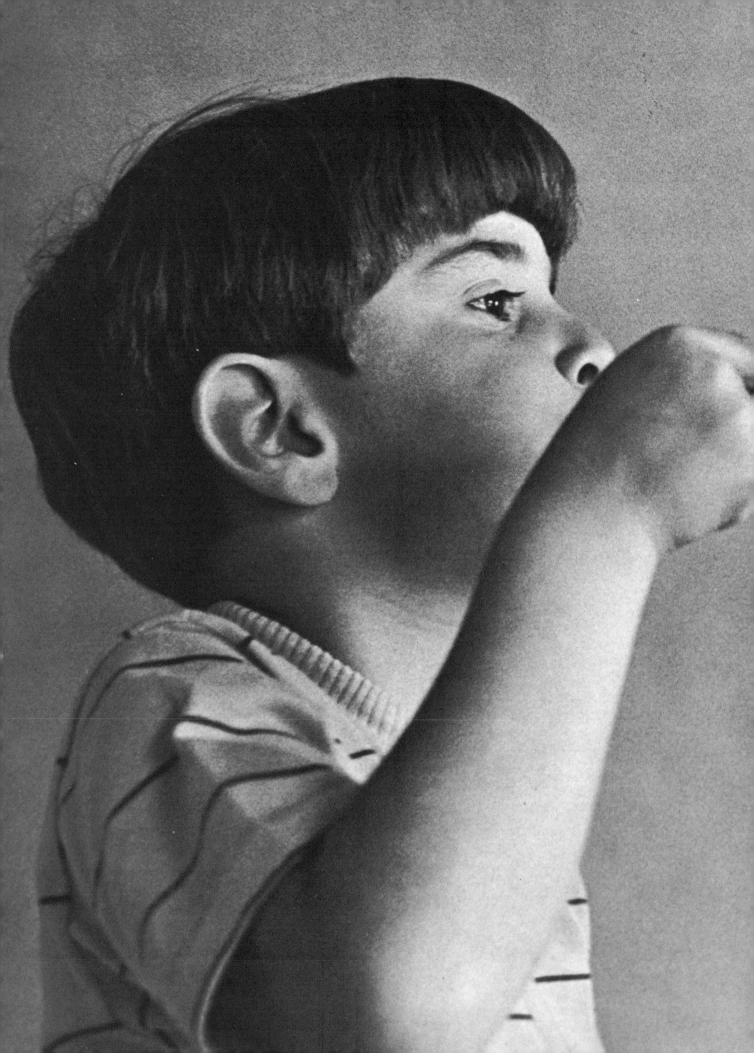

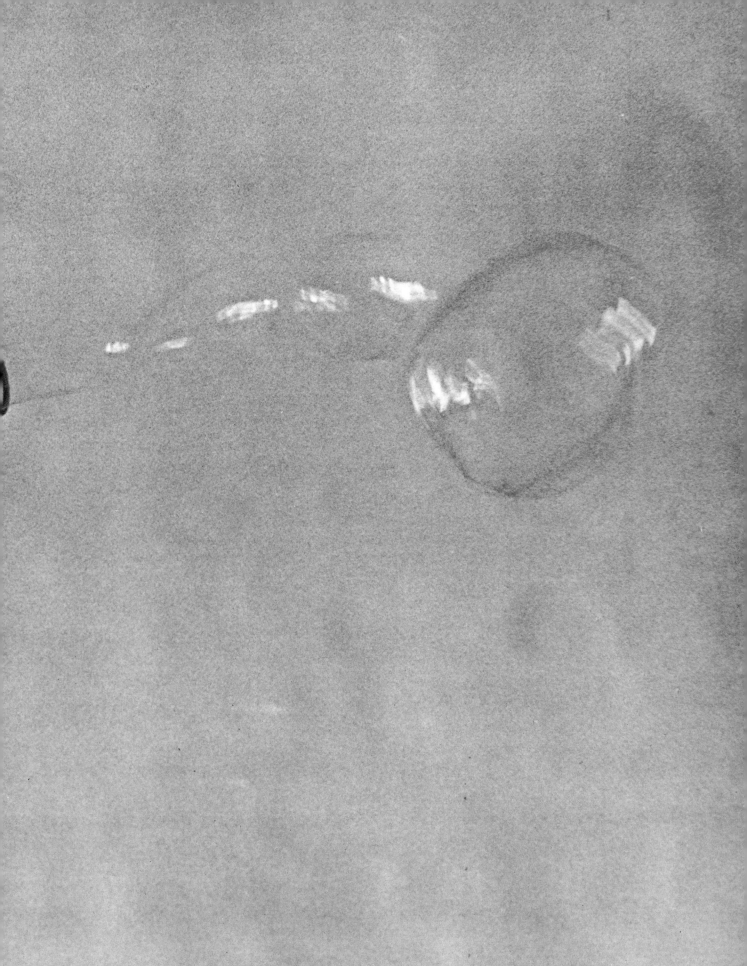

So much to do,

To explore,

To enjoy . . .

Like leaves,

Rocks,

The play of light,

Playing hide

and seek,

Preparing for sport,

Going fishing,

Looking for evidence of visitors from another planet,

Or finding out about the creatures on this one.

Their war games
are really games.

If they fight,

They make up easily.

Their boasts are idle.

Their hunting is harmless.

Their arms are open to the whole world.

They are addicted only to the heady pleasures of life itself.

ike going barefoot
through wild grass,

Finding a way
through the woods,

Rushing to grow up,

*Or practicing speeches,
getting ready to lead the world . . .*

But taking time to experience joy,

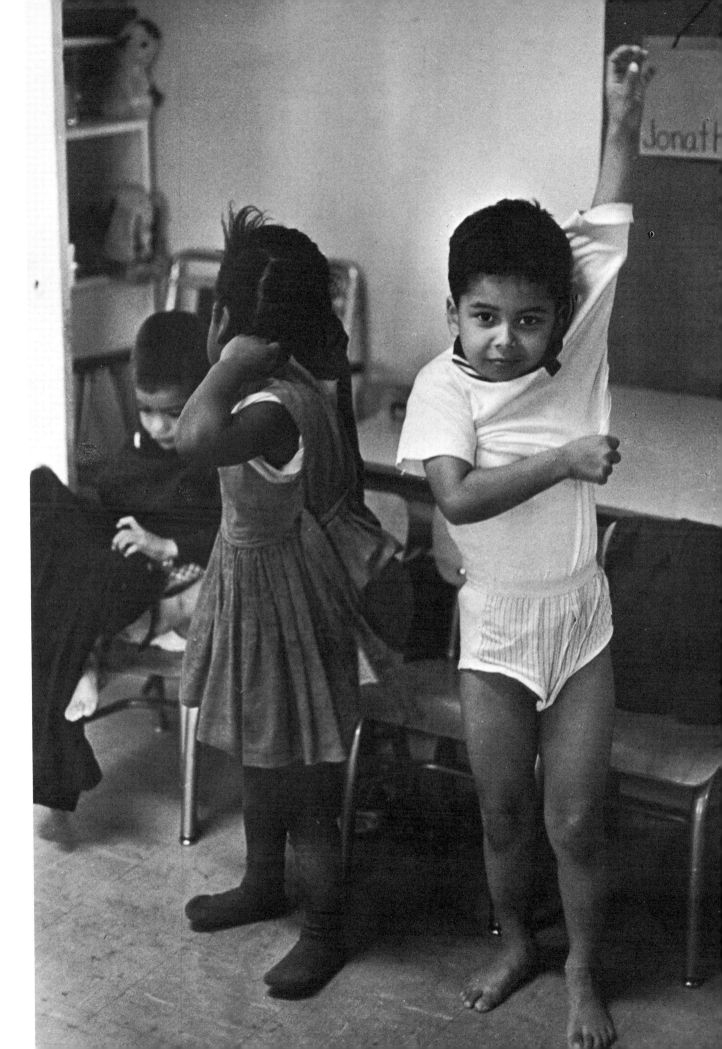

Each generation, time again is on our side.

Hope is in the children.

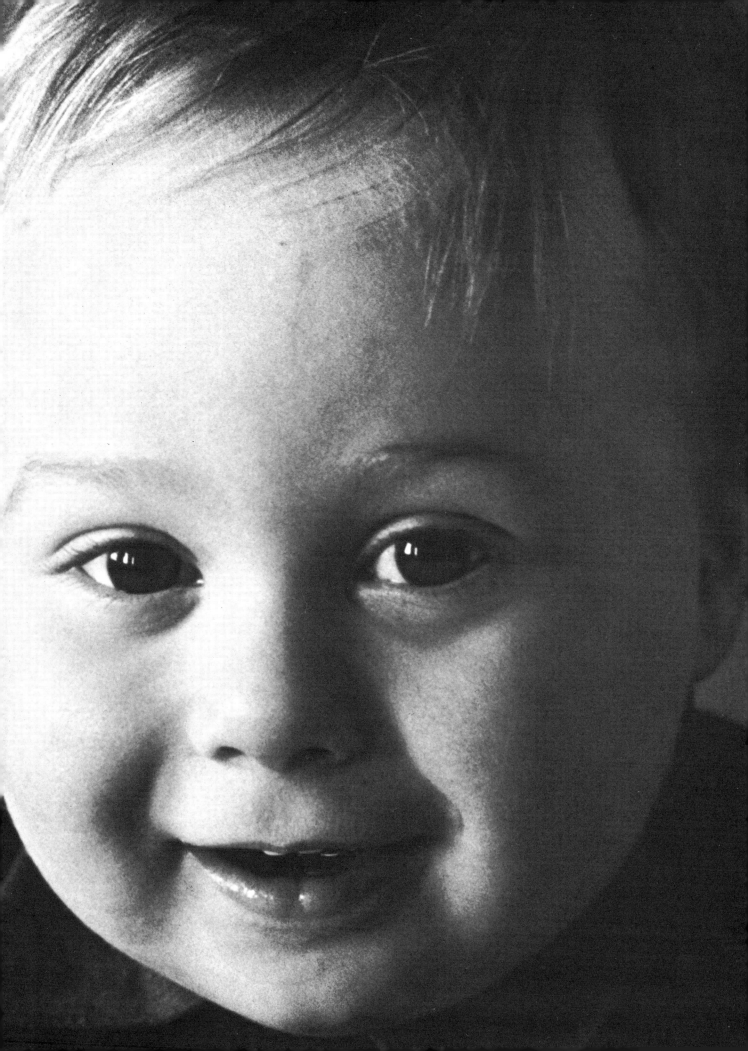